View From My Mother's House

CARL LEGGO

Sharon, (butala)
May these stories
of a mother's house
remind you of your
stories.
Carl Leggo
2007

View From My Mother's House

CARL LEGGO

killick press

an imprint of Creative Publishers

St. John's, Newfoundland
1999

© 1999, Carl Leggo

THE CANADA COUNCIL | LE CONSEIL DES ARTS
FOR THE ARTS | DU CANADA
SINCE 1957 | DEPUIS 1957

We acknowledge the support of The Canada Council for the Arts for our publishing program.

We acknowledge the financial support of the Department for Canadian Heritage for our publishing program.

I would like to acknowledge that some of the poems in View from My Motherr's House have been previously published in the following journals:

The Antigonish Review, Canadian Dimension, Contemporary Verse 2, The Cormorant, Egorag, English Journal, English Quarterly, The Fiddlehead, Grain, Landfall: A New Zealand Quarterly, The Literary Half-Yearly, The Newfoundland Quarterly, The New Quarterly, Pottersfield Portfolio, Whetstone, TickleAce, Windhorse Broadside: Poets' Choice: 1996, and *Update.*

Cover Art: Shawn O'Hagen (Subterranean, acrylic on canvas, 20"x30", 1992)

∞ Printed on acid-free paper

Published by

KILLICK PRESS

an imprint of CREATIVE BOOK PUBLISHING

a division of 10366 Newfoundland Limited

a Robinson-Blackmore Printing & Publishing associated company

P.O. Box 8660, St. John's, Newfoundland AIB 3T7

FIRST EDITION

Set in 11 point Centaur

Printed in Canada by:

ROBINSON-BLACKMORE PRINTING & PUBLISHING

Canadian Cataloguing in Publication Data

Leggo, Carlton Derek, 1953–

View from my mother's house

Poems.
ISBN 1-894294-06-8

I. Title.

PS8573.E461725V5   1999   C811'.54   C99-950109-7
PR9199.3.L3943V5   1999

For Anna and Aaron
who journey with me
in lines of connection
between east and west
writing the earth's light
in the light of the heart

Table of Contents

MY MOTHER'S HOUSE

Last spring I returned to my mother's house.
Like living in a Volkswagen van
each move had to be exact and slow and smooth.

My mother's house is a museum
of artifacts from Woolworth's and K-Mart,
every room crammed, everything in place.

My mother has two or three of everything,
just in case, because it was on sale,
because she found space not filled:

stacks of satin-bound blankets in cellophane,
more than the Glynmill Inn,
enough dish towels from Duz detergent

to wash all the dishes in all the restaurants
of Corner Brook, salt and pepper shakers
and pots pans mugs jars jugs cups cans tins

filling every cupboard corner crack cranny,
nothing ever used, just collected and stored
and protected like the treasure in Ali Baba's cave.

My mother's house is not a house
for dancing in, and yet I recall I once danced
in rubber boots. I was a Cossack from Siberia.

Every Wednesday night I wrestled
my brother in a match to the death
or the end of Skipper's patience.

My brother and I played pool in the kitchen
on a table with collapsible legs,
sometimes opening the fridge door to make a shot.

I was going to be the first Newfoundlander
to make the Canadian gymnastics team,
somersaults and handstands on the sofa cushions.

My brother and I shot ceramic animals
with darts from spring-loaded guns
like Hemingway hunting elephants in Africa.

But last spring in my mother's house
I was like a reformed bull who knows
how to behave in a china shop.

If I moved quickly I would upset
the balance. I learned to move little,
always slowly, but that is not how

I once lived in my mother's house:
    perhaps I have grown bigger,
    perhaps I have grown smaller.

EIGHT WINDOWS

north

growing up I saw
from eight lean windows
in my mother's house,
pitched in the gravel
of steep Lynch's Lane,
my whole known world,
culled in the compass
of the Humber Arm
and Long Range Mountains,
like a fortress,
and always I wanted
to see far beyond
the horizon,
the Atlantic Ocean
and the world Cabot
Columbus Cook wrote
in the maps of school
textbooks, but the first
time Skipper took me
cod-jigging, we sailed
past the Arm's curved line
where all I found was
the mirrored world,
refracted without end,
more of the same

northeast

a voyeur, I hid
like a pine marten
in a black-watch spruce,
unseen behind windows,
always frosted in winter,
spring oracular,
sun orange in summer,

autumn augury,
the harbour like steel,
the Humber Valley
unhinged and upside
down in the still water,
an image to be named,
but I could never
look, at least not much,
in people's windows,
always too much fear
about being seen,
as well as seeing,
like channel changing
the medical show
on cable TV
where doctors perform
bloody operations
on hearts and bunions

east

crow's wings line the fall light
of russet gold mustard,
while dogberries and blueberries
and damson and cherry
and crabapple trees
break the October frost,
with wind wrapped in whispers.
in winter I skated
to Summerside fast,
at least if the ice
breaker hadn't cut
the harbour in two
for cargo ships,
the rock and sky
and ocean no two days
in a row the same,
yet immutable

with cast centuries,
the tangerine sun,
harbour-held hidden
in the hills where
spruce pine light washes
the sky like an aquarium
conjured in fog ice fire:
the world born small

southeast

on Lynch's Lane we
always all wanted
to go some place else,
though we had a view
like tourist brochures
with salmon sun
splashed skies, ordered
with toll free numbers
in *National Geographic*,
like Gord Skiffington
went away to Toronto
returned every six
months with a purple
Plymouth Volare,
wide tires, jacked up back,
his mother's yard choked,
till others drove away
Gord's Volares seeking
Boston North Carolina
Elliott Lake Utah
Fort MacMurray Iran,
always returned, mum
about the places they
had found, said only,
I'm glad to be back

south

winter and spring storms
always washed Lynch's Lane
away, while workers
trucked tons of gravel,
and back packed ballast
and fathers even dug
holes under big boulders
and buried them deep
like they were planting
seeds to hold the lane
secure, though houses
stood firm on plots fitted
together like pieces
in a jig saw puzzle.
with no plan, the lane
grew hurly-burly,
broken and zigzagging
lines that wound around
long years of squatting,
twentieth century invention,
sewers, roads, utility poles,
and subdividing
for children who chose
their parents' backyards,
good a place as any

southwest

Carrie hung heavy
curtains, even sheers
like sieves to catch dreams,
poised potted African
violets and geraniums
on window ledges,
and refigured the view.
with the chesterfield
back against the window,

we gazed in the TV,
always on, bewitched
with *Happy Days*,
Honeymooners,
Hill Street Blues,
and Carrie remarking,
they are so bubbly,
it makes you tired
just looking at them,
all fictions of the world
outside the Arm's arc:
skits quips songs ads news
like the TV lamp
with a blue cellophane
train circling the heat
and light of sixty watts

west

June stung the eyes
with lime-washed picket
fences, yearly repaired
after the whole lane
winter-heaved, not sure why
we built fences, a gesture
of spaces claimed and named:
Baker Carter Collins
Downey Easton Feaver
Greene Hicks Janes
Jenkins Kennedy Leggo
Mosher O'Neill Pelley
Pike Pittman Purchase
Taylor Tobin Tucker
Warren Whiffen Yarn,
but no fence kept us out
since we walked free
wherever we wanted
through fences and tall grass,

nothing manicured,
wild flowing forget-
me-nots daisies
lupines buttercups
blue-bells clover over
running all our fences

northwest

a long time ago
I walked off Lynch's Lane
across the harbour
around Meadows Point
to live in Toronto
and other cities,
finally in Richmond
British Columbia,
a delta bordered
by a dike to keep
river and ocean out,
the only hills
stockpiled sand dredged
from the Fraser.
it's one thing to cling
to a valley wall,
another to live
in a world flat pressed
under gray soft skies,
seeking the same view
through eight lean windows
of my mother's house,
years ago bulldozed.
it takes a long time
to see the view whole

VERNA TIBBLE

Last night Carrie called,
Harry Tibble died.

He was repairing his roof,
died with a hammer in his hands.

Ready to shingle heaven now.
Poor fellow, you remember Harry.

Four, five years ago
Harry's wife Verna spent

all their life savings,
nobody knows how much,

on BINGO and lottery tickets.
She wasn't lucky.

She told Harry. The next day
she drove to George's Lake,

pinned the car keys to her coat,
nobody knows why,

and jumped through the January ice.
At the funeral, I said all I could say,

Harry, you must feel some awful.
Harry said, I just can't understand it.

How could Verna do it? How could
Verna spend all that money?

Last night Carrie whispered,
If Verna had kept her secret,

just a few more years,
Harry would never have known.

NO LOCKS

in my mother's house
doors had no locks

or we forgot to use them,
preferred, Can I come in?

the walls were thin like ice
on autumn morning puddles

no insulated world
the house never silent

the telephone rang
always TV glared

the radio chattered
records tapes blared

a little house
no space to hide in

no attic no garage
no storage shed

no hallway no porch
no upstairs downstairs

always somebody
dropping in

framed in the doorway
with jackets and boots on

No, b'y, I can't stay, just
wanted to see how you were doin'

oil furnace cutting in and out
steady hum in the long winter

the wringer washer twisted
a boiler of oil for chips gurgled

the refrigerator murmured
the fluorescent lights whined

clocks clicked
plumbing sluiced

always somebody going
and coming like a train station
like Tip the dog and his lover Ringo
who thought she lived with us

Skipper said, What are we doing,
heating up all Lynch's Lane?

everybody talked, all the time
at the same time

whether heard or not
performed soliloquies

a dramatic troupe
with kindled hearts

Skipper sang country and western
my brother impersonated TV stars

my sister was a feminist comedian
Nan improvised like Marlon Brando

I wanted to be Frank Capra
Carrie was the live audience

cars spun up Lynch's Lane fast
in order to keep traction

stones spinning
the mill steam whistle moaned

winter played the house
like a percussionist

the house always sweltering
summer night respite in the backyard

spring rain whistled
autumn wind teased

rhythms no poet could name
the house alive, breathed

people always calling to one another
always a sense of being watched

so close, smiling simultaneously
counterfeit and whole-souled
Carrie said, People lived close together
then, we'll never have that again

like she meant it,
like she missed something

CHLOE

just out of high school,
Chloe fell in love
with Jake, too many
matinees at the Majestic,
her mother muttered,
till a midsummer's night,
mid-sixties mania
even in the air
over Lynch's Lane,
Jake snarled,
Get out of my truck,
and so soon started
seeing Isobel,
and Isobel said,
I'm pregnant,
though she wasn't,
and Jake drove all
night the maze
of gravel lanes
in Humber East,
till morning when
he told Isobel,
Let's get married,
and Chloe couldn't
believe the way
the story was writing,
and got drunk
with Otto,
a few nights later
got pregnant
with Otto, too,
and Chloe and Otto
married the same day
Jake and Isobel
left Lynch's Lane
for good,
good riddance,

everyone said,
for Saskatoon,
while Chloe and Otto
walked Lynch's Lane
every day, at least
thirty-three years,
till Jake came back
to bury his mother,
and called Chloe,
who broke out of
the long dream,
leaped off Lynch's Lane,
walked out of the old
stories she lived day
and day with Otto,
woke up in Saskatoon,
not even a toothbrush,
with Jake who
she once wanted
always wanted, wanted
beyond all the telling

MY PROBLEM

After climbing Valley Road
one late spring evening
(summer anywhere else in Canada)
I sat with Cassandra
(seduced by my sixteen-year-old
imagination I had written
her the heroine
of my romantic stories)
on the back steps of her parents' house
looking for God hiding among the stars
and explaining why if I were American,
not Canadian, I would refuse
to fight in the Vietnam War,
and Cassandra said, I don't
want to go out with you anymore,
your problem is you want
to change the world.
I'm glad she told me.
I didn't even know
I had a problem.

THE SAME NOSE

Carrie says Skipper and I
have the same nose.

The son is in the father,
the father is in the son,
                perhaps.

Skipper daily disdains snobs:
Cobb Lane snobs, and snobs
who join, even want to join,
the Blomidon Golf and Country Club,
snobs who attend the Arts and Culture Centre,
snobs who moor in the harbour of Wood's Island
in big yachts to yak the weekend away,
snobs who eat at the Glynmill Inn
with prices three times higher
than the Seven Seas Restaurant,
snobs who drink coffee at the Natural Bean
instead of Tim Horton's (with dozens of donuts),
all the snobbish things I enjoy except
golf which I despise (even though
I've only ever played mini-golf twice).
Skipper snubs snobs with dismissive swipes.

Skipper's emotions wig-wag like a tall alder
in a hurricane shaken by hyperbolic currents:
Jobs? Things are so bad at the hospital,
you can be standing at the counter,
and the nurse admitting you will
receive a dismissal slip; she can't
even finish filling out the form,
she just gets up and goes.
Loud laughter like a gust of spring
punctuates Skipper's stories.
Carrie still responds, after all these years.
I grew up with a stand-up comic team:
George and Gracie, Lucy and Desi,

Ralph and Alice, Carrie and Skipper,
the busker, the jester, bursting out
always in song dance mimicry oratory.

Like a newsroom wire service Skipper
has information and opinions on everything,
especially municipal provincial national
international intergalactic politics.
Convicted truth shines hard in the air
around his head in concise editorial comments:
They think they're smarter than everybody else.
He's not right in the head.
They ought to put a bomb under his bum.
He never changes: father of the poet,
he offers me his stories, and stands still
long enough for me to know the poems.
He watches me writing in my journal.
It's all going down there now, he says.
He trusts me with his stories, even
invites the neighbours to read my poems.

The father is in the son,
the son is in the father.

Carrie says Skipper and I
have the same nose.

LINED LIVES

on Lynch's Lane
where I lived
in a house
with a back door
at ground level
and a front door
one story high
with no stairway
(you could walk
out the door
and fall
or fly away)
I lived winters
without end
in an iceberg
the world seen
in frosted glass
noting the sun
line the world
as I now live
in my poems
winter light
shapes of shade
l i n e
   s
w
  i
 r
l
parallel
 s
  k
   e
    w
concentric
  eccentric
where sun-like

I fuse
connections
line my life
live lines
without end

HOW BOATS ARE BUILT

I stamped through the spring
snow and mud to the shack of spruce
poles and plastic on the beach
where Uncle Jim built boats

but the shack was empty
except for juniper boards
and Uncle Jim in the corner
beside an oil-drum furnace
reading Robert Service.

What have you been doing
all winter? I asked.

Just sitting in this corner, he said,
watching the alders grow in the ice,
trying to stay warm, dreaming
the new boat in the air.

It's almost time to call
the woods together. Soon.
Already I've sailed a sea or two.

LOTTERY TICKET

Like a seagull scavenging the shore for scraps
I turned again to my mother's house in search
of still more stories, though I long thought I'd written
all the stories of Lynch's Lane, learned instead stories
always end in et cetera, like rain in Vancouver.
My brother flew five hundred miles
to spend five days, the first in five years,
came I assumed with a store of memories.
I was eager to listen, to receive gifts of stories.
I called my brother my research assistant.
We drove the autumn circle of the Bay of Islands.
What do you recall? I asked. He was silent.
Finally he said, Nothing. Perhaps I was asleep.
I told him about playing cowboys, about how
he and Cec argued about who shot who.
He said, I think it was you who argued.
I poked, Recall how you mimicked Chanel No. 5 ads,
whispered with weary French worldliness,
It's not easy being Catherine Deneuve, left eyebrow
raised barely. I think I saw his eyebrow hover.
My brother sat in a corner of our mother's sofa,
watched the movie channel, scratched lottery tickets
without end, counted wins and losses, always zero.
While I seek a fictional past, he seeks a fictional future.
He flew back home, and phoned the next night,
perhaps scared by the stories I might write out of
silence, perhaps eager to set the record straight,
said, It was fun, still held his stories sacred.
Like tuckamore I cling to the granite edge of memory,
while my brother lets the past pass like gallstones,
his stories stored in an iron urn buried in his backyard.
I am a poet pushed off shore in a punt with no oars.

LESSONS FROM CHILDHOOD

Tobey Buffett stuck a pencil
up his nose and poked out his eye.
We called him Cyclops,
and for a quarter he'd peel back
the white gauze bandage his mother
taped to his face every morning,
and show us his eye like a dried apricot.

First time I saw her in kindergarten
I fell in love with Bonnie Lee Sweetland.
For almost a decade I knew
I couldn't live without her.
In grade eight I asked her to a movie.
She said yes, but I didn't have
enough money for two tickets.
In junior high she was in a different
room in a different world. Last time
I asked anybody about her, they said
they hadn't seen her for years.

Uncle Rube wore gold wire-rimmed glasses
and never washed behind his ears.
His glasses rubbed the side of his face away,
right to the bone. Cancer ate him up,
the neighbours said, with loud sucking
noises like a vacuum cleaner,
and every day when the teacher inspected
my fingernails, I always got gold stars.

My father met Cyril
outside the Caribou Tavern,
Sorry, Cyril, to hear about the old man.
Cyril's eyes blue like the bottle caps
on Blue Star beer smiled
at my father not smiling
(it's not every day a man dies).
Yes, Skipper, he's gone, gone for good,

22

and you know, he left a whole sack
of potatoes and nobody to eat them.

Uncle Abe spread out his hand
on the birch chopping block
and challenged his sister
to chop off his hand.
She lifted the axe high
over her head and whacked off
two fingers which she glued
back on with spruce gum.
Uncle Abe could still use them
though his sister stuck them on crooked,
and they felt like alder sticks on his knuckles.

PORTRAIT OF THE POET AS A BABY

even at six months
my mother tells me
I stood in my crib

one night she peeked
into my bedroom
sure I was asleep

only to find me leaning
on the crib rail
like a passenger

on a cruise ship
waving an olive hand
that had found

a hot muddy place
inside my diaper
and had scratched

on the blue wall
like a vertical sea
lines of shit:

even then one of us
knew I would grow up
to be a poet

HUSBANDS

when her husband died
on Valentine's Day,
thirty-three years together,
Winnie Gullage said,
No man will ever put
his hand above my knee
again, but by summer's
end, she was seeing
Ned Baldwin for chips
and beer at the Summit,
and by Thanksgiving married
Ned, and in a gray spring
buried him without flowers
with the same incantation,
No man will ever put
his hand above my knee
again, and married Gil Burt
who lasted a few years
only, worst of the lot,
some said she said,
but still in her eighties,
much to her eldest son's
dismay, married Abe Pike
who she always grinned
was the only man
who ever knew
how to love her

ALIENS

in elementary school I chased Betty and Janet
in go-go boots like Nancy Sinatra wore
and nylons that crumpled around their knees
not knowing what I'd do if I ever caught them
once slipped into a storm sewer ditch spring swollen
Janet laughing as I tread water and tried to grin
once almost caught Betty but knocked her down
and broke her collar bone   for years
I was in love with Betty and Janet but I can't
remember their playing with Cec Frazer Macky
my brother and me   can't remember if they ever
tobogganed or built tunnels in the snow
or erected forts or joined our snowball battles
remember only the icy storm sewer ditch   Janet's
loud laugh   the tear of pain in Betty's face

CROQUET

Mel Mercer built the first patio in Humber East,
a rectangle of concrete slabs no bigger
than a family cemetery plot, and he built
the first barbecue, too, an oil drum cut in half,
filled with charcoal briquettes, and all summer
long he called the neighbours together
to sip Scotch and croon with Perry Como
and eat tenderloin steak wrapped in bacon.

Billy Mercer sat on his verandah in the dark,
rocked in a white wicker chair, and watched
the parties on Mel Mercer's patio, more
fun than anything on CBC, he said. Even
though Mel Mercer always waved, Join us,
Billy Mercer wanted only to watch, knowing
the see-saw balance between nephew and uncle
augured accurately the alignment of planets.

But everything changed the forest fire summer
Carrie counted her Gold Stamps from Coleman's
where every payday she picked up groceries
and burned a Gold Stamp shopping spree
like a winter-crazed prospector across the catalogue:
lawn chairs, plastic tumblers, a card table.
Everything we wanted Carrie got with Gold Stamps,
till there was nothing left to get except a croquet set.

A few times I had seen croquet played on TV,
aristocratic, civilized, genteel, British, but
on Lynch's Lane with no level yard for croquet,
we had to pound the wooden balls up the hill,
nudge them down the hill through stubbles of grass,
and never smack the balls into Skipper's rows
of potatoes. Everything connected, like one ball
conking another, Carrie's croquet convened chaos.

Day after day Billy Mercer watched us play croquet.
So his daughter bought him a set at Canadian Tire, but
Billy Mercer wanted what no one on Lynch's Lane had:
a level front yard like a TV suburban manicured lawn.
He worked out the mathematics (asked to help, I
nodded at his sketches with my grade nine geometry)
of moving the back yard to the front yard, and excavated
and dumped tons of clay and rock, a new Antaeus.

Mel Mercer looked out his kitchen window
and saw a wall of grass and gravel like a tsunami
poised to crash on his patio. Angry hot, he told
anyone who would listen, some who wouldn't, all
the stories best kept between uncles and nephews,
stories bumped stories, the hard crack of croquet balls
caught in the slate gray sky over Humber East, echoes
off a patio, verandah, yard, now always winter empty.

PIRATE'S TREASURE

Dale's father
(small and dark like Errol Flynn)
sometimes sold men's shirts
door to door
on the Great Northern Peninsula
from Bonne Bay to Griquet
but mostly dressed in pale pink shirts
and mornings
paraded down Lynch's Lane
and Old Humber Road
to the Caribou Tavern
and afternoons
visited Mrs. Birch (tea, Dale said)
until one blue afternoon
Mr. Birch (uninvited)
joined Dale's father
at tea with Mrs. Birch
and the hill was a bonfire of curses
when Mr. Birch
thrust Dale's father
(bare feet, gray pants, no pink shirt)
high above his head
and twirled him round
and round
like a helicopter
ready to fly
(Dale's father was no Errol Flynn)
and sparks of silver
change flew
and Cec, Frazer, Macky,
my brother, and I
looted a pirate's treasure
of nickels, dimes, quarters
and bought hard candy
(three for a cent), bags full,
sucked all day
and still had some left
for tomorrow

THE POET OF LYNCH'S LANE

Cal Denney was the only poet
I ever knew on Lynch's Lane

pissed Gloria Pike's initials
in the snow, once even her whole name

pricked SHELLEY TRUE LOVE on one forearm
with a darning needle and India ink

carved YOURS FOREVER in hearts
in desks, his, mine, others

spray painted MY LOVE IS A ROSE
on the limestone cliff above Ada Dunphy's

wrote LO   VE on his eyelids flashed
at girls and boys he said were girls

spelled I LOVE YOU in beer bottle caps
hammered into a girlfriend's fence

or shaped in jelly beans or shoestring licorice
or stray pulp logs at Wild Cove

STITCHES

Cec Frazer Macky my brother and I all had
fathers who took us to Wood's Island jigging for cod
drowned cats in jute sacks over the Ballam Bridge
cut waist-high grass with sighs of the scythe
clung to tall ladders to screw winter windows
planted potatoes and pumpkins in backyard plots
shovelled snow like Charlton Heston riving the Red Sea
disappeared to the paper mill or cement plant most days
repaired houses fences appliances during holidays
sputtered through teeth-clenched mouthfuls of nails
always with the same puzzled look on their faces
like they didn't know what planet their sons had come from,
often said, I'll be some glad to go back to work
where I won't have to listen to your whining and warring

like the time Chip came back from Brampton and spoke
with an accent even though he'd been away a year or two
only, grew up on the hill at least a decade, and we tried
playing with him, but babble about Brampton baffled us,
till Chip's father muttered to our fathers how Chip had
nobody to play with, and Skipper complained we ought
to play with Chip since he was just back for a week or two,
and we were playing war with scrupulously scripted rules,
but Chip insisted he played with Brampton rules
and launched a rock grenade which exploded fire
in the back of Cec's head and blood ruined his St. John's
souvenir T-shirt while Cec's father and Skipper rushed Cec
to emergency where he had at least twenty-five stitches
and the nurses gave him popsicles and dixie cups all night

under a full moon with tides tugged and harbour swollen,
Skipper, ready to burst, barked, I'd like to get my hands
on that damned crazy kid from Brampton, threw a rock
big as a boulder, nearly knocked Cec's brains out his ears,
stay away from him, boys, he's dangerous, he's lunatic,
and with the opaque heaviness of our father's words
riddled with overwrought cracks like spring pond ice

Frazer Macky my brother and I stood like caribou frozen
in a car's headlights, not knowing what to do for Cec or Chip,
and we craved the clear advice of our mothers who alone
somehow always knew how to stitch the parts together
whole so the world made sense, seemed seamless,
and years later when I heard Chip died in a plane crash
I felt bad like the story was unravelling still

NAN'S BROOCH

My grandmother could never understand how
young women could kiss old men on *Another World*.

Oh, that old thing. She loved Bob Barker
like she loved salt, ordered from Carter's Store

pickled pig's knuckles, herring and turbot,
sneaked salt meat into the pot when Carrie wasn't looking,

laughed over salt cabbage, craved salt
like winter-starved deer on *The Forest Rangers*

where Gordon Pinsent, the only Newfoundland actor
we knew after Joey Smallwood, took care of the world,

while my brother and I resurrected Camelot in blankets,
our grandmother trapped in a kitchen corner

with a cup of tea, nowhere else to go,
till the crash of knights in battle left her

a damsel in distress. I'm going to tell your mother,
as soon as she gets home. She never did.

One Christmas I gave my grandmother a sterling
silver brooch from Silver's and Sons on Water Street.

I asked Mr. Silver to engrave the back,
        I love you, Nan,

words I'd never said to my grandmother, though
at sixteen, home just left behind, I wanted

to say the words. I gave my grandmother the brooch.
Read the back, Nan. She rubbed her eyes.

She couldn't see the words. Carrie read the words.
We all smiled. Always so many silent letters

in our story, but in the back of the brooch, concave,
I saw my grandmother and me upside down,

as I ride vertiginous each day a playground ride
spinning on an axis while I cling to the edge of a circle

and remember my grandmother who lived in the margins,
never in the world, never out of the world,

brought to her by neighbours, TV, and *The Western Star*,
and our final New Year's Eve, long ago, not so long ago,

when I stayed with my grandmother while Skipper
and Carrie went to a party. I slept in my old bed.

When the year ended with gunshots and pots,
I found my grandmother scratching the floor.

I picked her up. I put her back in bed.
I tucked the blankets in tight under the mattress,

the way my brother and I once built Camelot.
After decades when she seldom left the house,

my grandmother in her last year was bent on escape.
I didn't tell Carrie. My grandmother never told on me.

MOOSE

Skipper tells me
a long time ago
Cousin Ty shot
a moose,
quartered it,
and hung it outside
his cabin door
while he played
poker and drank
Captain Morgan
with his uncles
Bull, Eddie, and Max,
and around midnight
stepped into the clear
October air
under a full moon
and stars beyond
counting, but
could see only
a dark hole,
no moose,
and the whole world
was condensed
in a black circle
from which Cousin Ty
hurled words
like silver missiles,
for weeks
accused everyone
of stealing
his moose,
buying, eating,
freezing his moose,
knowing who stole
his moose,
bought, ate,
froze his moose,

and when Bull,
Eddie, and Max
tried to cool him
down, Cousin Ty
shot at them, too,
accused them even
in words of fire
drawn from the earth's
center, words long
buried, resurrected
words, that burned up
a store of memories
like photos
curling to black ash,
and when Bull died
Cousin Ty wouldn't go
to the funeral,
and when Cousin Ty's
daughter married,
only the groom's
family attended
in a lop-sided church,
but Skipper
doesn't know what
Cousin Ty said
to his uncles
and he doesn't
want to ask

THE POSTER

my first semester away from home,
still sixteen, living with Tony
in a narrow rectangle in Bowater House,
Memorial University of Newfoundland
now almost the whole universe

I bought a poster at Woolco:
a black and white photo of a stream
running through a copse of conifers
sketching the sky, overlaid with words
I cannot remember, but words

jammed with enough emotional energy
fired in the poster frenzy of 1970 when
religion was both waning and waving,
almost everyone in Bowater House came
to my room like a shrine, sat on my bed

and scribbled the poster words to send
to parents and girlfriends, to pin up
on bulletin boards over their desks
where they could be daily sustained
with a handful of heartful words

I wrote my parents, and eagerly
included the poster words, handwritten
in my plain clear style, but I hadn't learned
the MLA style for including citations yet,
still a semester or two away

soon after a note arrived from Carrie:
We read your letter and we couldn't
make any sense out of it, you wrote about
settling in and receiving the parcel I sent
and the next thing we know

you are talking about being one
and serene with the sky and water
and trees, and Skipper and I were sure
you must have been on drugs
when you wrote the letter

I learned how dangerous it is
to write, how often language baffles us
with Hermes playing his confounding
tricks, and so I gave up sending
my parents words, too worrisome,

but now almost three decades later
in poems I am beginning to say
again what I always wanted to say,
but still I send this poster poem
with a clear message:

I am not on drugs,
only possessed with poems

GRADE FOUR GEOGRAPHY

(for Aaron)
In grade four geography
I read about
Bunga the Pygmy
who lived in Malaysia,
and other children, too,
tucked away in faraway
corners of the earth:
the steppes of Russia,
the savannahs of Africa,
the outback of Australia.

In grade four geography
I saw illustrations
of ten-year-old children;
for all their differences
they looked the same:
like Barbie dolls
with interchangeable costumes.

In grade four geography
I memorized enough
lists and facts
to colour the earth.
For example, what foods
did Bunga the Pygmy eat?
Mostly yams.

In grade four geography
I knew the earth
was an object,
solid, stable, static,
easily described,
the earth present
in the words
and pictures and maps
of my textbook.

In grade four geography
I learned about Bunga
the Malaysian Pygmy
who ate yams,
but I never learned
what Bunga learned
about Carl the Newfoundlander
who ate the tongues
of cod dipped
in milk, rolled
in flour, grilled,
light brown, crisp.

In grade four geography
I never saw Bunga
looking back at me,
perhaps asking,
How can he eat
those tongues?

MY SISTER AND HORACE

once upon a time a long time ago
I went away and left my sister.
she grew up and I knew only
I didn't know her, never would.

one Christmas or one spring
I returned with a hippopotamus,
stuffed jelly bean stripes.
she named him Horace.

she grew up with Horace, at least
until its fuchsia tongue spoke
no more about coconut chews,
philosophy, and Charlie Brown,

and one day wrote a poem
about the death of Horace,
now too grown up for a funeral.
perhaps I died too

because I lost my sister
and search for her in photos
where she rehearses roles,
no false smiles for the camera.

instead the camera smiles for her,
reflects images readily missed
by the eye, true images, no cheese,
and find my sister in this poem,

my sister who once loved me,
and Horace wrapped in plastic,
hidden in a basement closet,
preserved by our mother.

LIMING THE FENCE

Lilly Mercer celebrated
her golden wedding
anniversary with a little
speech: Sam, I can't stand
anymore, I'm leaving you,
and marched up
Lynch's Lane
to Skipper in the yard
liming the fence,
and told him
what she was doing
and said she hoped
Skipper would look
in on Sam sometimes,
mostly bed-ridden
since his left leg,
black with gangrene,
had been amputated
and his liver,
pickled in rye,
had been condemned,
and Skipper visited
Sam later that night
with a box of Turtles,
and they ate chocolate
caramel pecans, biting
the legs and heads off
first, through Bob Barker's
Truth or Consequences and
Rowan and Martin's *Laugh-in*,
and Sam was handling
the marriage break-up
with a wry grin: Skipper,
she up and left for devilment,
but he didn't complain
about Lilly's defection
as if he knew he deserved it

and died two weeks later
leaving a note:
Skipper, tell Lilly
I died with a broken heart.

I don't think Skipper
ever told her.

NAN'S SOAP

February, another storm,
the whole world sculpted
in snow ice hibernal world,
we huddled in houses
watching *Another World*.

Sharpe's General Store
exploded with Guy Fawkes'
volcanic vision, the hot heart
of a glacier, gutted, charred.

all Lynch's Lane Harbourview
Bannister's Old Humber Road
charged through the snow to shop
in Sharpe's surprise spree.

awash in the crowd's wake
Nan and I, lunatic looters too,
except Nan barred my way
to the charcoal castle in ice,
everywhere danger lurks.

she showed up with Sunlight soap,
chair legs, seats, backs,
not enough for a whole chair,
a pale gash in her sooty face.

it's the place that we know only
between dreams and nightmares,
she said, it'll take all the snow
on Lynch's Lane to clean our loot,

but let's go again anyway.
see if we can get the parts
to make a whole chair, perhaps
two chairs even, be nice to sit
and watch *Another World* together.

LIGHT SNAPS

once I saw Delia Greening
in the window of her bedroom
in a pale pink negligee
like the inside of a Hawaiian conch.
for weeks I sat outside her window
but never saw her again.

Mugs O'Keefe was a witch.
she dressed in black long overcoats.
I can't remember her face.
she was Dale's grandmother.
we played baseball in her backyard.
sometimes she gave us candy.

when Maisie Bannister complained
to her cousin Benny Bannister
that his new fence cut off four inches
of her land, complained daily,
he punched her in the face,
and paid the magistrate's fine.
best fifty dollars I ever spent, he said.

one spring Carrie mixed a concoction
of oil and iodine and basted herself
in the sun till her skin turned pumpkin.

Sophia sailed from Bulgaria,
expecting a groom in Montreal,
but was enchanted by autumn
fire in the Humber Valley and
asked no questions about winter.
everybody at the Caribou Tavern
fell in love with Sophia,
but no one more than Nick
who picked a fight over darts
to prove his devotion.
with his jaw wired,

he sucked soup through a straw,
held by a tender Sophia.

at nineteen I told Carrie I was getting engaged.
she said, I don't know what your father will say.
he said, you're old enough to make your own decisions,
though he didn't sound very convincing.

Henry was Chinese.
he owned a confectionery.
after a long time, a wife
came from Hong Kong.
she was much younger.
when Henry died, she ran
the shop for decades
and never spoke
a word of English,
just smiled and gave us
what we pointed at.

when Nan heard the Pope had died,
she said, his wife must feel some bad.

on Lydia Lake's wedding day,
her father got drunk
and punched the best man
who punched him back, hard.
Lydia Lake's father lost his left eye.
at least the marriage lasted a long time.

Saul Gillam announced
he was leaving Lynch's Lane
to find work since Knowlton Nash
had just reported there were
a thousand jobs in jeopardy,
though he wasn't sure
where Jeopardy was.

when Christina Kelly married Mel Musseau
she made him sign a prenuptial agreement
like they were in Hollywood or Brunei.
after she had three children, she dumped Mel.
she only wanted me for one thing, said Mel.

Madge Gullage left the cover of her mailbox
up as a signal to Vince Hicks
that Nels Gullage wasn't home,
but surely Nels suspected something
with Vince walking up and down Lynch's Lane
a hundred times a day waiting for the signal,
everybody glad when he finally went in.

Dottie Dove had a black baby
for a cook on a Bowater's cargo ship
who sailed in and out of the harbour once,
the only black baby in Humber East.
he grew up to be a basketball player.

when the Jehovah's Witnesses knocked,
Carrie always bought *The Watchtower*
and left it in the bathroom
with *Real Confessions* where
I could order glasses
with X-ray vision.

about a week before the Herdman graduation
Jake Wheeler wanted to impress Julie Johnson
and drove his car fast at the Western Terminal wharf,
but his foot was welded to the gas pedal
and they splashed into the harbour and drowned.

Cec's mother put on a bathing suit
and came and sat in my brother's lap
and had a Polaroid snap taken.
she brought me raisin bread.

after years of pining
I had my first date with June,
beautiful like a summer day,
but that morning found
a big cold sore
like an unripe crackerberry
in the corner of my mouth.
I couldn't kiss her, I never did.

my brother once saw April Rose
dance the Sultan's Feast at the Caribou
with Roy Orbison on the juke box,
stopping only to plug more quarters.
nobody much cared after years
of stripping without surprises,
but my brother plugged quarters for her.
he claimed April Rose danced
like a Persian princess.

by the middle of August I could pick
enough blueberries in the rocky cliffs
near the CBC station to fill most
of a mason jar and Carrie always said,
I think there's enough for a pie.

Dale's mother was the first person
I knew who died with cancer.
she organized birthday parties.
now a lot of people are dying with cancer.

every Christmas Mrs. Gillam baked
cakes for the neighbours, dark and light
fruit cakes, with a hint of Jamaican rum
to add a little equatorial cheer,
and her best friend Molly Dwyer
always ordered a couple dozen
for her sons and daughters
and their sons and daughters,

but just before Christmas Mrs. Gillam
died, and her daughter phoned
Molly Dwyer, Mom is gone,
and Molly Dwyer replied,
I wonder how I can get my cakes.

when Dallas, who Carrie said was gorgeous,
went to Fiji with Dr. Boland the dentist
and married him, no one even mentioned
the first few husbands, but Carrie mused,
there's something about people down the coast,
they have a different attitude towards it all,
they take life more easy.

Mrs. Coughlan sold me fatty beef
because she knew I wouldn't complain,
and always made mistakes in arithmetic
when writing my bill with bright teeth.
I learned how to read smiles from her.

when Lilly Ledrew won the lottery,
she bought the Caribou Tavern, and
in the first few years Louie Ledrew
drank the profits and died.
Lilly said, like winning the lottery twice.

getting older
like everybody else,
says Carrie,
in light etched lines.

REVEEN

a long time ago, every Saturday,
Cec Frazer Macky my brother and I
went to the Majestic Theatre
for reassurance that John Wayne
was still keeping the world safe
for democracy and decency,

but one Saturday the Majestic
trembled when Reveen
the Mesmerist in a purple
sequined tuxedo jabbed a sharp
goatee with the precision
of Sigmund Freud and bobbed
a perfect puff of black hair
like Wayne Newton: Las Vegas
and Venice, incarnate in Corner Brook.

we watched people who believed
they were apes spies astronauts boxers
run dance hug laugh wake up
and return to their seats
where with a word from Reveen,
they bounded up again to obey
his commands. while I laughed loud,
I wasn't brave enough
to be hypnotized.

a few nights ago my daughter saw
Reveen at the Queen Elizabeth.
he still wears the same
purple tuxedo with sequins
from thirty years ago, the same
goatee, the same puff of hair.
he still conjures the same stories.
like me, my daughter was enchanted.

she stayed after the show
for Reveen's autograph.
he said, you'll sleep well,
and you'll never have any desire
to smoke. she was pleased,
but I'm worried about Reveen.
I sleep well and I don't smoke,

but I burn with morning desire
to write poems, make up stories,
conjure with words. the real
world always feels unreal.
perhaps Reveen mesmerized
me with promises I would
grow up to be a poet.

I hope he reads this poem
and learns how dangerous he is.

BULLIES

Libby Sheppard and Eddie Russell
were hard cases, always in trouble,
hoodlums like Bonnie and Clyde

neighbours said they never took baths,
their mothers served them sugar cereal
and white bread, three meals a day,
they drank beer, smoked, and had sex
like wild goats, all the time, in the woods

Cec Frazer Macky my brother and I
spent all Sunday planning and building
a snow fort we called Fort Knox, only
to watch Libby and Eddie knock it down,
and I said nothing because once I chased
Libby, and she just stood and waited
for me to catch up with a wolverine's
fierce eyes, so I went home

I remember little about Libby and Eddie,
they were the dark creatures that hid
under our beds, trusted only to play their roles,
the world then in balance for good kids,
our mothers' warning in our ears and hearts,
Do you want to be like Libby and Eddie?

Eddie went to reform school and became
a bouncer in a bar in Barrie while Libby,
sixteen, married an American sailor
and went to live in Hawaii, like scapegoats
sent outside the walls of the neighbourhood

JESSIE EZEKIEL

when the ladies
from the Mission League
visited Jessie Ezekiel
she served them tea
(like Saturday night
bath water, said one
of the ladies) made
with one used tea bag
because all her life
Jessie Ezekiel hoarded
her money (millions,
Cec said, hidden
in the basement) and went
to the Glad Tidings Tabernacle
and sat in her backyard
knitting Phentex slippers
for the heathen in Africa
and not once ever
asked us to go
to the store for her
and one August afternoon
Cec, Frazer, Macky,
my brother, and I
were waging the war
to end world war
and I saw Jessie Ezekiel
climb a ladder
to her roof (always
dabbing black glue;
used tea bags, said Cec)
to stop leaks
and I aimed my rifle
at the enemy
and shot her once
through the heart
but she didn't fall
because her lead heart

couldn't be pierced
and I crawled
through the grass
seeking more enemies
when I heard
a loud gulp
and saw Jessie Ezekiel
flying falling
like an angel
testing her wings
and in her will she gave
all her pinched wealth
of ninety thousand dollars
to the Mission League
and a dollar each
for the children
on Lynch's Lane
to buy candy
at Carter's Store,
but when I sucked
the peppermint knobs,
jujubes, and toffee,
I couldn't tell
anyone I felt sick

SKIPPER SAVES COPPER COOPER

one Tuesday in July
Copper Cooper went away.
goin' troutin', he said.
Thursday morning, his mother,
perched in the kitchen door,
woke all Lynch's Lane:
COPPER'S LOST
                COPPER'S LOST

Skipper took the day off,
joined Alphonsus Pardy,
walked the woods and hills
all day, round and round,
wouldn't stop even to eat
a can of Vienna sausages,
while mosquitoes ate him,
his face alder whipped

Alphonsus read every
broken branch like a book,
and blew on the barrel of his
shot gun like a trumpet.
the blast, Skipper insisted,
could have heralded
a moose to heaven and glory,
but not Copper Cooper

Skipper stumbled through
the dusk to his Valiant,
a note on the windshield:
we found Copper Cooper
around eleven o'clock,
see you at the Caribou.
Skipper said, we couldn't find
him because he was found

that night all Lynch's Lane
danced in the Caribou.
Ned Cooper, Copper's father,
grinned and hugged Skipper,
Holy Jesus Mary and Joseph,
give Skipper a drink,
today he saved my boy Copper
and I loves 'im for it

Skipper drank his rum,
scratched mosquito bites,
smiled at Copper's father
out of a chokecherry swollen
face, drank more rum, tried
to remember the last time
he'd even seen Copper Cooper,
at least last Christmas

JULY PATCHWORK QUILT

1

marsh marigold maidenhair
aaron's rod chuckley pear
bachelor's button bakeapple
bog lily pond poppy
bottle brush beaver root
swamp thistle dandelion
lupin laurel lady's thumb
polypudjum pitcher plant

2

through
weeping willows
the sun sets salmon
pink mauve lavender
the evening star
in an orange sky

3

gulls
shrawking   scraping
like unoiled machinery
beseeching
keening

4

lemonade quenching
the fire sunburned
from the inside out

5

w
a
t
e
r
f
a
l
l
line without motion

6
above the ocean, almost
still, a gannet hangs still
alone

7
capelin weather
foggy cool wet
airsome

8
fir
aspen
juniper
alder ash
spruce pine
poplar balsam
tuckamore birch
oak
elm

9
a fat man
sleeps in tall grass
his stomach erupts
from pants and shirt
a roll of white flesh
like yeast-raised dough
before kneading

10
tickleace murre
swallow curlew
linnet dovekie
ptarmigan gull
partridge puffin

11
the ocean gargles
sloshes   roars
distant cannon-fire
lullaby

12
Coleman coolers lawn cots
cotton candy coconut
patchwork quilts popsicles
plastic alligators pop
frisbees flies french fries
Scotties chips rubber dinghies
Noxzema baby oil band-aids

13
the sand always moving
rolls over feet
into mouths and eyes
hides in hair

14
t
he
hori
zon
a
lon
g
scri
bbled
lin
e
dra
wn
w
it
h
eye
s
clos
ed

15
all the bathing suits in Sears catalogue
planted in the cold water of Deer Lake
daisies daffodils hockweed hollyhocks
pansies peonies petunias sweetpeas

tulips violets lilies clover bleeding
hearts begonias bluebells buttercups

16
mist clings to the water
tangerine ocean waves
toasted almond beach sand
myrrh of evergreens lime
spruce air lemon breeze

17
blue taupe gray green
hemisphere
sky beach lake hills
etched in aqua sunshine

18
out of the sky
clouds have fallen

black crepe draped
over the hills

darkness moves
over the land

19
bodies lie in the sand
dried capelin
codfish split cured
boiled lobsters

20
through bare birch branches
the bald blue mountain

21
mottled green hills
black-watch plaid
shadows alive
in the hills

22
an old woman
throws a few handfuls
of sand on her grandson
buried in the beach

23
s
l
i
v
e
r
of
s
i
l
v
e
r
moon
pinned in a purple sky

24
blue sky
paler   blue
near the   horizon
deeper blue   as you reach
into the top   of the bowl

25
berries
blue partridge stew
rasp goose dog squash
cran cracker caribou
berries

26
laughter, midnight echo
of the brook

27
in a world of
v
e
r
t
horizontal
c
a
l
lines
skewintersecting
the road is a
ser
pen
tine
sc
ra
wl

28
boys fishing
from the wharf
connors flounders
catfish sculpins

29
children playing catch
kick-the-can cricket
grounders red rover war
like crackies barking

30
the sun
a capsule of cod liver oil
light glinting off
the steel blue sea
molten lead

31
a boy about ten pulled from the water
a lifeguard trying to inflate
the still purple carcass
clouds hiding
the sun

BLUE STAR

on a January morning
Tommy Samson challenged
Cec, Frazer, Macky,
my brother and me
to a test of manhood:
one who keeps his hands
in snow longest wins
a medal, promised
Tommy Samson who packed
snow into the holes
our hot hands melted,
and Frazer gave up
quickly as he always did
and Cec had to go
to the store for his mother
and Macky who wanted
licorice went with Cec
and my brother heard
my eyes shout,
chop my hands off
before I give up,
and went home
to watch TV
(he didn't like
beating me anyway),
and my hands were mottled
pink blue white like opal
when Tommy Samson
carefully removed
the cork liner
from a Blue Star
beer bottle cap
and slipped a fiery hand
inside my shirt
to press the liner
against the cotton
into the cap held

on the outside,
to pinch the medal
in place over my heart,
the only medal I won
from Tommy Samson
because in the spring
he fell off the log boom
in Deer Lake and drowned,
though years later
I'm still competing
for Blue Star medals

ROSALIE POLLETT

Rosalie Pollett crawled out
her bedroom window to grass
with Jed and Frank and Pikey,
and sometimes Jed let
Cec, Frazer, Macky, my brother
and me sit nearby and listen
to Rosalie moaning in the alders
like a spring northeast breeze,
and at fourteen Rosalie had
what Carrie called a moonlight child
which the Salvation Army took away
since Rosalie was a child, too,
and her mother was dying
in the sanatorium with tuberculosis
and her father dressed daily
in a navy three-piece suit
like a banker, not a bank's janitor,
and at eighteen Rosalie married
Gerald in the Canadian Armed Forces
and everyone on Lynch's Lane
got drunk with joy for Rosalie
going to Germany with Gerald,
but Rosalie hadn't realized
how big the world really is
and at twenty disappeared
while Gerald wrote letters
all over the world searching
and at twenty-one Rosalie came back,
a changed woman, saved and cleansed
in the blood of Jesus, she said,
and at twenty-two Rosalie returned
with Gerald to Lynch's Lane,
and everyone got drunk with joy
and we were still celebrating
when Rosalie crossing Humber Road
on her way to Lockyer's Store
was run over by an ESSO truck

THE POET IS A POEM

(for Al Pittman)

You were the first poet
whose voice in my ear
was not alien.

More than two decades ago
I heard your voice
like a homespun sweater.

When I started writing long
after English teachers told me
I'd never be a writer,

your voice sang in my head,
wove words with my words,
savory on the tongue.

For years I felt
your breath in me,
echoes in my ears.

So you could not know
how much your words
of praise meant to me

when my first book was born
and you swung to the center of the atrium
like a loose-limbed scarecrow,

and nobody knew what you were doing,
crashing the party perhaps,
and you sang the notes

scribbled at the Columbus Club
after hearing my poems on the CBC,
and a circle was formed

from the first time I heard you read
to the first time you heard me read,
our voices, one voice.

On a plane from Corner Brook to Vancouver
I held your new poems and wept
with dancing in limbo.

Months later you came to Vancouver,
a city with too many polite poets,
to the Writers' Festival.

You began with a funny aside,
too much laughter, the audience
unsure how to read you.

I wanted to stand beside you,
welling up with words, and whisper,
our voices are one.

I wanted to put my arms around you
and ask you to recall the words
you had spoken about my poems.

I wanted to read one of your poems:
the house burning or no one calling you home
or refusing to give your daughter away.

I know you hear the rhythm
of your voice in my voice,
the voice you gave me long ago.

But I couldn't move:
I am too polite;
I do not know you well enough;

I have no right to butt in;
I would cause a scene;
I am too polite.

I did nothing.
As always, I did nothing.
All alone, alone.

Your ten minutes were almost up
when you regained your voice,
gruff and rough and sweet.

And, Al, on the stage, alone,
hundreds of people staring,
people you knew were there,

but couldn't see, blind with light,
you read a poem about being alone,
you were a poem about being alone.

I wept as I read your new poem.
I weep as I write my new poem.
The poet is a poem.

A STRANGE TONGUE

on Lynch's Lane Ralph was a comedian,
a kind of Henny Youngman or Jack Benny
with one-liners like machine gun fire,
and like Red Skelton he told his stories
with so much eagerness to please, people
laughed even after years of repeating,
and Millie laughed most, The silly old thing,
she called him, until one night
Ralph left the Caribou Tavern
because they'd run out of Old Sam,
said he was going next door to the Legion Club,
walked several blocks thinking
next door was a long way,
walked into the Glad Tidings Tabernacle
with the after-service in full swing,
a noisy party of crying singing testifying,
got himself saved and baptized
with the Holy Ghost, babbling away
in a strange tongue the pastor said
was praising God (gibberish, mumbled
the teens huddled in the back),
and they filled the baptismal tank
behind the pulpit, dunked Ralph in,
and he danced home wet in the cool July air
singing, When the saints come marching in,
Do Lord, O do Lord, O do remember me,
more drunk with Jesus than he'd ever been
with Old Sam, and always he asked,
Have you been washed in the blood of Jesus?
I don't want to be lonely in heaven,
Have you been touched by the hand of God?
You can't arm wrestle Satan on your own,
the clown converted into a ghoul: a night
out, now a wake at Fillatre's Funeral Home,
Sunday afternoon strolls in graveyards
and visits to the hospital to see the ones
everybody knew wouldn't be going

home again, though Ralph sometimes
slipped into the maternity ward to tell
mothers, The poor little creatures didn't
choose to come into this corrupt world,
and Millie crumpled her eyes:

I know Ralph loves God, but
how can God love Ralph?

ALL HALLOWS HALL

fixed in a triangle of grass
no one wanted to mow
with winding wild rose bushes,
a squat gray building
at the junction of
Dove's Road
    Fudge's Road
        Old Humber Road

All Hallows Hall was hallowed,
the one place where
Protestants and Catholics
forgot they were
Protestants and Catholics

where mothers played bingo
and drank Red Rose tea at craft fairs
and sold one another slippers
in Phentex wool no sheep would wear

where fathers squeezed in to watch
Clobie Tynes imported from Halifax
to play hockey for the Royals
box anyone foolish enough, Dale's father
beat up so many times people moaned
when he volunteered again

where the whole hill gathered
for baby showers church suppers
wedding receptions union meetings
bake sales Weight Watchers
political rallies Girl Guides

where on rainy Saturday mornings
I first saw Ulysses outwit the Cyclops,
John Ford reconcile ranchers
and shepherds in the wild west,
and Jason and the Argonauts
search for the Golden Fleece

but when I returned last
Halloween like Ulysses
after the longest journey, all
I found, where All Hallows Hall
had been, was a hollow
and a highway, even
the wild roses are gone

APPLES

Georgie Fiander loved apples
(especially stealing apples)
and climbed Mamie Jenkins'
picket fence of sharp spruce spears
(the kind Borneo headhunters use)
and climbed Mamie Jenkins'
tree into the September sky
high above our heads,
was swallowed by the tree
(Mamie Jenkins boasted it ate boys)
and the metallic blue air
rained apples, green, hard, sour,
till it seemed we would drown
in a flood of apples
(Cec laughing because
Mamie Jenkins was faraway
at bingo and couldn't shoot
us with rock salt)
and Georgie Fiander was
wringing the storm cloud
till every last apple dropped
and we heard the sharp
crack like a rifle shot
and the charge through the branches
and Georgie Fiander fell
in a shower of apples
across Mamie Jenkins' picket fence
and when we pulled him off
his face was shiny apple green
and Georgie Fiander ran home
holding his ripped stomach
(we knew he wouldn't be eating
apples for a long time)
and three days later Mamie Jenkins
stood at Georgie Fiander's grave
and her green face shone with tears
like an apple on an October morning

A TROPHY

instead of hanging out in Gushue's Pool Hall
where most of the boys squandered their mothers'
quarters in pinball machines, instead of stealing
empty pop bottles from Hank Hicks' truck
while he delivered Coke to Carter's Store,

I signed the Salvation Army temperance pledge,
learned catechism for Sunday School,
memorized English kings and queens,
and tied enough knots for Boy Cubs
to win the Outstanding Cub Trophy for 1962-63,

and for years I stood like the loin-clothed
golden figure with arms stretched high,
a torch in one hand, lined abdominals,
screwed to a wooden platform, even
Baden-Powell would have been pleased,

till one summer Saturday night I lingered
on West Street with Janet and Betty
under a full blue moon, drank too many Coke
floats, and sneaked into the dark back alley
behind the Humber Pharmacy to pee

when a Royal Canadian Mounted Policeman
stormed up in his cruiser, jumped out,
like he was Mannix or Cannon,
barked, stretch your arms high, over your
head, lean against the fence,

and I was the trophy figure, stiff, arms
outspread, oblique, as he frisked me, like I
was a Hell's Angel, snarled, next time,
find a public washroom, and I leaned on the fence
a long time before I climbed Hospital Hill,

still longing to be the Outstanding Cub
I couldn't tell Carrie, waiting, sipping Nescafe
at the kitchen table, her first words, what's wrong,
I said nothing, with tears pushing hard
against my face, the trophy jammed in my mouth

GOOD ADVICE FOR POETS

Under a harvest moon
Uncle Hollis dropped
in on his way home
from an AA meeting
at All Hallows Hall,
explained to Carrie
how AA members tell
stories to one another,

therapeutic tales,
retracing past
journeys in order
to write the future
more hopefully,
sobering stories,
seeking contexts
for present texts.

Uncle Hollis said,
People have terrible
tales to tell.
I can't repeat them,
I wouldn't want to,
but it's no surprise
they sought comfort
in scotch and Old Sam.

Uncle Hollis asked,
Can you remember
anything terrible
that happened to me?
I can't, said Carrie.
Me, either, said Uncle Hollis.
In fact, said Carrie, I think
yours was a charmed life.

Uncle Hollis agreed, I was
adored, got away with lots.
Carrie smiled, Remember
the winter you built
an ice rink in the basement?
Hollis laughed, When the ice
melted in the spring I raised
chickens down there.

Uncle Hollis sighed,
I'll just have to tell them
I lived a charmed life.
Yes, said Carrie,
you can't make up
stories that show
people as cruel
when they weren't.

NEIGHBOURS

1

our neighbour Cal Petley
dug a ditch late at night
while Skipper slept
and buried a drain pipe
that ran into the high grass
in the upper corner of our yard
and for days drained his sewage
until Skipper mowing the grass
smelled his neighbour, said
nothing, just plugged the pipe,
and Cal Petley mopping the floor
around a blocked toilet, said
nothing, just ran a longer pipe
into the town ditch

2

our neighbour Billy Mercer
excavating his basement
asked Skipper if he could dump
some fill in our yard,
mostly unused potato plot,
and Skipper said, Sure,
and Billy Mercer dumped
all the sifted stones
late at night when everyone
ought to be sleeping
and for days we could see
him peeking out his curtains
to mark if Skipper was going
to throw the stones back

3

our neighbour Georgie Snooks
dropped into the house
every night on his way home
from the Caribou Tavern
and sat at the kitchen table
talking about the weather and darts
until he was sure his wife
was asleep, but after years
of late night conversation
Skipper found it harder
and harder to find
anything to talk about
and just let Georgie Snooks
watch television

4

our neighbour Tommy Winsor
(in delivery dropped
by a drunk doctor)
slept and smoked and shrieked
on his mother's verandah,
spent one day shaking
his big red penis at everybody
going up and down Lynch's Lane,
spent the next day preaching
to everybody going up and down:
Repent, you goddamned sinners
bound for the fires of hell,
except Skipper who he always
asked for cigarettes

5

our neighbour Sterling Earle
collected bottles and coins
outside the Caribou Tavern
while his mother having forgotten
him spent most days and nights
in the Glad Tidings Tabernacle
and ordered Lick-a-Chick chicken
for Lillian, the last of seven,
the only favored, while Sterling
and his brothers and sisters
found bread and grace, here
and there, where they could,
and Skipper dropped coins
near the tavern entrance

LOST MOTHER

May March once lived
alone in a shack
of tar paper mill-cloth felt
at the top of Lynch's Lane
in a triangle of tall grass
roseroot and dandelion
lined by fences of neighbours
who couldn't remember who
owned the wedge of land or
how May March came to be there

alone she spelled tales of husbands
stolen to groves of witch-hazel
where she conjured a moss child
fairied away, years away, no one
knew where, till one day he tracked
his way back in a summer blue
suit with sheila's brush erasing
the lane in still another winter burst,
and the lost son of May March
asked Nan for his mother

with each question Nan's eyes
watered as if whipped
with a blasty bough,
I don't know, my boy,
and May March's son said,
ma'am, you don't know much,
and Nan whispered, most
of the time I just make stuff up,
but this day I wish only I knew
how we lost your mother

FAMILY TV

TV fathers sipped
martinis at day's end,
wore suits to work,
solved all problems
with quick quiet words,
and lived in rooms of their own:
studies dens rec rooms
bedrooms with single beds
where they wore pajamas

TV mothers read
thick novels
under bedside lamps
after sipping
percolated coffee
all day, mostly sat
around with other
mothers talking
about the mothers
who weren't sitting
with them sipping
percolated coffee
all day

watching TV
I wondered
who I could be
in another
                family

my mother father
brother sister
grandmother me,
familiar and unfamiliar

I often tried
to convince
my brother
he was adopted
because I could
convince my brother
to believe anything
and I wanted
to know the limits of
            anything

but perhaps in my family
we were all adopted,
strangers washed up
on Gilligan's Island,
longing for rescue,
Lost in Space,
seeking home,
Hogan's Heroes,
prisoners waiting
for war's end,
the Beverly Hillbillies,
aliens making the best
of an odd world

in my mother's house
I saw TV
cannot contain
the limits of
            family

WHO WERE YOU?

(why I write poems)

as the sun swings from equinox
to solstice Lou Gushue strolled
up and down Old Humber Road
like he was the baron of a fiefdom

Carrie always said, He's a good
man but no good to work,
wants only to be a gentleman
with two dollars in his pocket

last summer I squat in the unmowed grass
where my mother's house long stood,
when Lou Gushue stopped, so I said,
I grew up here, now I'm writing poems

Lou Gushue sighed, Who were you?
Leggo, I smiled, with a peasant's
resignation to ingratiation, and
Lou Gushue squinted, Leggo?

my father was an electrician
at the mill, walked this road
to and from work for forty years,
almost as often as you, I laughed

Lou Gushue looked out the bay,
Are you sure? Seventy years ago
I was born on this hill, never left,
but I don't recall any Leggo's

THE MEANING OF X

well Carl my son

I had to write ye a few lines its in the night now I am bad enough in the day I suppose ye are getting settled away by now we had a lovely day here today how is poor Kathy Wendy got her jacket come it is some nice she loves the school not a bit strange ye think she was going all the time she takes her dinner ye know what she takes tin of drink pack of chips cheesies bar comes home filled right up she bars herself in her room to learn her lessons you know theres nothing undone the only thing she dont stay up so long in the night I suppose poor Paul is all dried up by now I dont know if I told you that Jerry is going to St Johns Friday on the bus there is two or three of them going poor fellow Effie said she didnt like to keep him from everything he is coming back on Sunday I dont know what time he will get in but one of them got a sister there but he will be right up with ye and Willie your mother told him to go in and stay there on till ye comes he will see Sandy when he gets there first I guess she will go with him to show him where ye are to Fanny said she didnt see ye when she was away I guess that ye were out somewhere your mother and father was some glad when they got their letter and ye know your grandmother wasnt sad Ringo stays in where Wendy is learning her lesson in her room it wont be too long please God before ye will be home for a little while some good remember me to poor Kathy your mother takes her little walk same as usual so long

Nan xxxx

BLUEBERRIES

a few years ago
Lynch's Lane disappeared
in urban redevelopment
      knocked down homes
      dispersed people
      asphalt highway
but stored in my eyes
are memories:
in the weekend
between summer and autumn
Skipper filled the Nash
with buckets egg sandwiches
Kool-Aid children wives
(his and neighbours')
wound out of the city
around the south shore
      Mt. Moriah
            Frenchman's Cove
      John's Beach
            Benoit's Cove
      Curling
            Blow-Me-Down
all day in air scented
spruce salt heather-moss
we picked blueberries
tumbler into bowl into bucket
gallons of blueberries
everywhere blueberry
pies grunts crumples
even eyes asleep
were blueberries
e v e r y w h e r e
blueberriesblueberriesblueberries
stamped on the inside
and outside of my eyes
stained in blueberry juice

WINTER ALPHABET

returning in March after seven years
of November to January rain

I know only I have forgotten
the winters I grew up with

for a few days I walk in Corner Brook
as if I am fighting winter

head down, going somewhere fast
except I move slowly

almost pantomime, pushing myself
through winter like walking under water

I must learn to lean with winter
seek its erratic rhythms

like a dory sliding up and down
the smooth sides of a rough sea

I taste winter, winter savours
my body with a lustful lover's appetite

snow bites pinches pokes stabs
slices like a set of sharp knives

in a TV infomercial
neatly skinning a tomato

snow acts with verb exuberance,
a veritable thesaurus of action words

winter reduces the world
people stay home more

huddle in their cars more
hide in shopping malls more

deep snow, hard-packed snow,
plowed snow, powder snow

no hint of spring anywhere
except spring always comes

sunglasses essential, blind colour,
light and shadow tear the retina

snow in mountain creases
and cracks, a monochrome world

like the alphabet on paper,
a text I am learning to read again

reminded how quickly I grew
illiterate, lost my language

CUL-DE-SAC

Skipper and Carrie now live
in a cul-de-sac in a white house
with a garage, neighbours they visit
at Christmas, a level backyard

with a picnic table, a manicured
front lawn, shrubs and flowers
along a walkway to the back door,
a basement, warm and dry as upstairs

a porch dining room cellar workroom
den rec room laundry room hallway,
a second bathroom with a walk-in shower,
even more rooms they never use

in my last visit I told Skipper, I'm going
to walk on Lynch's Lane and record
images in my journal, and he said,
when we moved we lost our view

a big loss, I agreed, there's not
a lot to see in a cul-de-sac
where windows reflect other
windows in a circle, but

Skipper didn't sound unhappy,
more matter of fact
like he was reminding me
you can't have everything

COAST LINES

I

after years of watching
Wagon Train, I knew
the lure of the west, and so
left the east, left the west
coast of Newfoundland
for the west coast
of Canada, always
westward to

the edge of morning
where a heron stands still
in the slough near the dike
I walk daily, gulls hang
in the sky, a sea lion
spills with the river,
an eagle watches
from the tallest alder

while I too wait
and watch, my image
upside down in the smooth
Fraser River, all the world
topsy turvy, but
still in balance,
I learn to be still, even
in a whirling world

on the edge of the day I
dance and laugh all the ducks
in the slough in the air,
our wild line scribbling
writes the earth, writes us
in the prepositions
which connect all
the parts of the sentence

2

always the earth
moves all ways:
seasons like arms
of a windmill,
moon-tugged tides,
morning never far
from evening light,
shadows in a tangle
with the sun,
the weather at least
as chaotic as life
itself, the wind
bearing earth's breath
always familiar,
always unfamiliar,
no two days the same

I must learn by heart
the earth's rhythms,
eager to write the light,
in aspens alders apples,
like an eagle gull heron
writes light in its flight,
sees the world
from other locations

knows the world
written in difference
where I linger on the edge
of the Pacific Ocean,
calling out the view, far
from my mother's house,
seeing still all the world
through eight windows